HELLO HOLIDAYS

FLOWER ART AND INSPIRATIONAL QUOTE DESIGN

STRESS RELIEVING & RELAXING COLORING BOOK FOR ADULTS

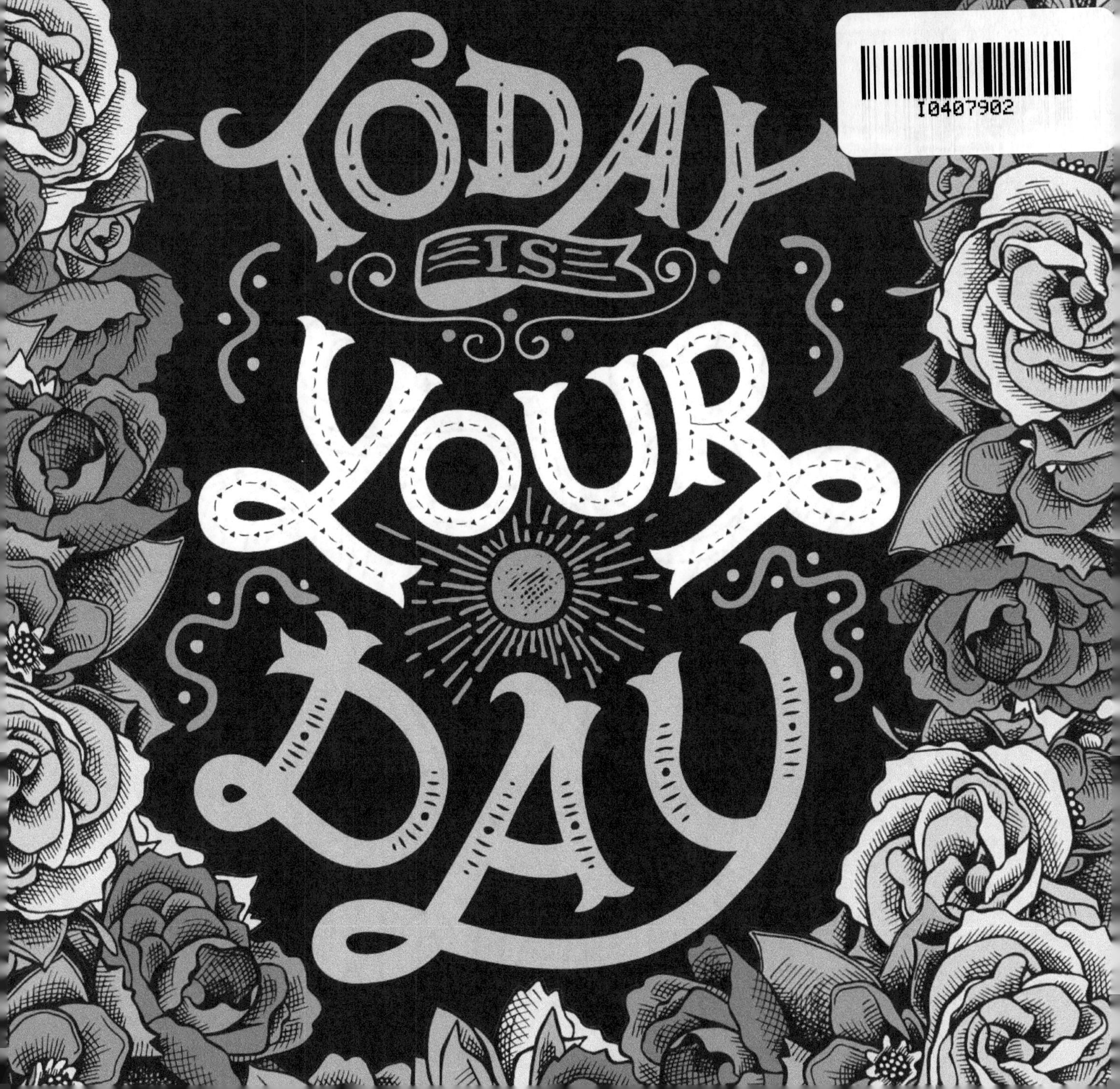

life is short
AND THE
world
IS WIDE

You're so amazing

life is short
AND THE
world
IS WIDE

HOME IS WHERE
the heart is

LIFE IS SHORT
enjoy your coffee

life is short
buy the shoes

you're
so
pretty

congratulations

life is better
WHEN YOU'RE
laughing

life is better
WHEN YOU'RE
laughing

ALL YOU NEED IS
ice cream

hello monday

we can dance
FOREVER

Wake up
-AND-
smell
the roses

hello
new day

LIFE IS SHORT
choose happiness

you're
so
amazing

shoes speak
louder
then words

www.ingramcontent.com/pod-product-compliance
Lightning Source LLC
Chambersburg PA
CBHW081604280526
45788CB00011B/3548
* 9 7 8 1 5 4 6 7 6 6 3 8 4 *